Solving the Cross-Work Puzzle

Solving THE CROSS-WORK Puzzle

Succeeding in the Modern Organization

Robert P. Crosby

VIVO! Publishing

If you are interested in more information or would like to discuss the concepts presented in this book, please contact:

Crosby & Associates

West Coast: 206.369.9200
East Coast: 302.983.1429
or online at: www.crosbyod.com

Book Layout and Design: Gayle Goldman Graphic Design
Cover Illustration: Damon S. Brown

Library of Congress Catalog Card Number: 94-79823
ISBN-13: 978-0-9776900-1-5

Acknowledgments

I doubt that this book could have been conceived without Kurt Lewin's seminal work in the first half of this century. His classic statement that *Behavior is a function of the person times the environment* is the fundamental formulation upon which this book rests.

I am also indebted to Paul Brainerd, founder of Aldus Corporation, who sponsored my work at his innovative company where cross-functional product development was a way of life.

Although the words and concepts are mine, I am so fortunate to have many skilled people who have made the final product tangible, attractive, and readable:

- A special thanks to my friend Doug Smith for help with the vignettes and the photo which appears on the back cover.

- Terry Schmidt's editing job truly enlivened the text.

- Graphic designer Gayle Goldman and cover artist Damon Brown have placed these ideas into a very attractive package.

Thanks to Michael Heinrich, for his editing. Mike's touch graces this book in ways that only an author can know.

Contents

Figures

Dedication

To Patricia Nordby Crosby,
mayá zhina e kalyéga (my wife and colleague),
as I so often affectionately say in my street Rus-
sian. You are deeply experienced and so highly
skilled in "doing" what this book is all about.
And thanks for suggesting the title.

Preface

This book tackles one of the most critical puzzles facing people who work in organizations today: how to turn out quality work on time and within budget as a member of a networked or cross-functional task force, project, or product team. Classic project management components omit critical elements necessary for success in the emerging virtual and complex organization.

As the global economy evolves and competitive pressures rise, companies large and small must discover more effective ways to organize to get cross-functional work done. The traditional hierarchical model which served so well during the industrial era has become obsolete. In the simple 19th-century model—borrowed from the military—work was done within a single supervised unit and most communication occured *within* work units.

That model—one of vertical hierarchies and decision-making based solely on position in the chain—is inadequate for these times. In the evolution between the old and the current ther was a gradual introduction of "projects" or "product development matrix groups." Decades ago they were not the normal way of doing business rather, there were a few projects living in the traditional organization. Classical project management practices were sufficient. Companies in the '90s are far more complex. Today, tasks crossing organizational lines are the norm rather than the exception. In such cross-functional organizations, most if not all, work is done across, rather than within, functional units.

As tasks and communications cross department lines, success demands a new approach suited to the complexity of cross-functional forms of organization. What you are about to read is just such an approach.

There are three dimensions critical for success in cross-functional systems. These three dimensions are

- human interaction patterns,
- task component clarity, and
- organization health dimensions.

This book concentrates on the first two and provides an instrument for measuring the third.

In the pages that follow, you'll discover the skills and strategies used by the best leaders in solving these "cross-work puzzles." You will learn how to balance the key task skills with essential human interaction skills and, in so doing, guide projects to successful completion.

I've written this book for project team leaders, members, and senior executive project sponsors who are willing to pay attention to key systemic problems, significantly involve workers/ employees, and lead in a clear way. These are people willing to be clear about their own wants, able to connect with others, and able to handle resistance without blaming. They are active advocates for change who are willing to "bite the bullet" and be decisive. If this description fits your aspirations as a leader, welcome to *Solving the Cross-Work Puzzle*. Read on!

Chapter 1: **Sorting Out the Puzzle Pieces**

"When ALCOA began feeding production data
back to the factory floor, workers at its
Addy (Washington) plant quickly saw ways
to boost productivity by 72%."

—BUSINESS WEEK, JUNE 14, 1993.

Can productivity really be increased as much and as fast as the *Business Week* quote implies? Can merely feeding production data back to workers quickly boost productivity by 72%? Is that all it takes to get significant, sustainable performance increases?

It's seductive to believe that quick fixes will yield such dramatic improvement. Unfortunately, the reports of change that appear in the media are often superficial and focus on the "miracle cures" of empowerment, quality circles, self-directed teams, TQM, and currently, "re-engineering." These reports do a disservice to all of us. Like many of the faddish weight-loss schemes on the market today, they encourage simple solutions and new "programs" instead of undertaking the longer-term systemic change (which may include some of those programs) necessary to develop a healthy structure.

I have passionate opinions about this topic because I was an important player in the Addy turnaround which *Business Week* described, and I believe that the media quote oversimplifies the causes of the increased productivity. From 1990 to 1992, my colleague and wife, Patricia Crosby; internal ALCOA consultant, Tom McCombs;[1] and I spent more than four-hundred days assisting in the Addy turnaround.[2] Key to the success was an unusually clear and effective plant manager, Don Simonic. The ALCOA plant at Addy had initiated "self-managed" teams in the mid-'70s. By 1990 it had long-since been suffering from the maladies of that approach, perhaps not unlike Volvo's short-lived experience at the "self-directed" Uddevalla Plant in Sweden.[3]

The major focus of our work at Addy was to increase cross-functional effectiveness. Without considerable improvement in this area and the ability to handle projects, I do not believe the success would have either been achieved or sustained.

Projects: They're not Just for Engineers Any More

As we approach the 21st century, more and more organization work is done through projects that cross functional lines and traditional disciplines (engineering, marketing, manufacturing, sales, finance, etc.). Learning to master projects—both as a project leader and team member—is an essential bedrock skill for the future.

Projects come in all types, shapes and sizes. Chances are that much of your professional and personal life consists of doing projects. At home, undertakings like remodelling the guest bedroom or upgrading your home computer system are typical examples. At work we might see a hospital task force bring a new maternity service on line or another accomplish a wholesale revision of a university curriculum. Projects can be defined as organized efforts to accomplish specific goals within a defined schedule and budget. People in the work arena have difficulty at times distinguishing them from ongoing operations, but projects have clearly identifiable characteristics. They:

- focus on achieving specific, important goals,
- involve the coordinated undertaking of multiple, interrelated activities,
- have a beginning and end point (though some matrixed or cross-functional groups are permanent),
- are often highly visible and political,
- typically involve a new configuration of individuals who must work together as a team.

As the business environment becomes more complex and organizations require better approaches, project teams, committees, and cross-functional task groups are emerging as the most important mechanism for getting work done.

Evaluate your own work life and you likely will conclude that much of it is already project-based. Expect that trend to accelerate. Tom Peters described future organizations consisting of "networks of projects." More of the work that's mission-critical, innovative, and future-oriented will be accomplished through projects carried out by cross-functional task forces and temporary teams.

The Rise of Cross-Organization Structures

The traditional way most companies organize is along "functional" departmental lines. A quick glance at their organization charts depicts major functions such as engineering, operations, administration, research and development, human resources, information systems, finance, and others. Within each of these functions is a further breakdown or grouping based on the type of resources available or the type of work done. Finance consists of accountants, tax experts, financial analysts, and so on, while Marketing may include advertising, market research, sales and public relations functions.

This organization form was well-suited to the days when the business environment was simpler and less volatile. Most work was clearly compartmentalized and could be accomplished within a single department. Marketing marketed, engineering engineered, manufacturing manufactured, and there was little need for them to interact. A functionally-oriented management style worked well in that environment because the organization structure was relatively static and roles didn't significantly change.

But as the world rapidly becomes one global marketplace and competition increases exponentially, the functional structure is ill-suited to many organizational tasks. The need to develop and produce better new products less expensively and get them to market sooner in a faster moving world of complexity demands solutions by teams from across the organization. Companies are discovering that their most critical projects require a mix of diverse, specialized skills from workers representing a variety of departments. In many cases they will work together on a short-term basis and then disband. At other times, they may fill an unmet organizational need so well that the *ad hoc* task force is consciously given permanent status.

Such matrixing or cross-functional arrangements have grown in number and will become inevitable as managers discover the old models to be ineffective. Pretending that most decision-making in these new arrangements can be consensual is as obsolete as it is to be authoritarian most of the time. **There is a middle approach that does not deny the reality and the need for both authority and serious input from all relevant parties.** Under these new structures, projects usually borrow their staff from the functional departments on a temporary basis. Some organizations, however, have restructured with (formerly) functional employees newly organized as perma-nent units with, for instance, engineering, production, mainte-nance, and marketing workers reporting to the same boss and in the same unit. This restructuring solves certain dilemmas and, of course, inevitably creates new ones. No matter how one organizes, certain issues must always be addressed. We will deal with these in the upcoming pages.

Figure 1 Cross-functional or Matrix Structure

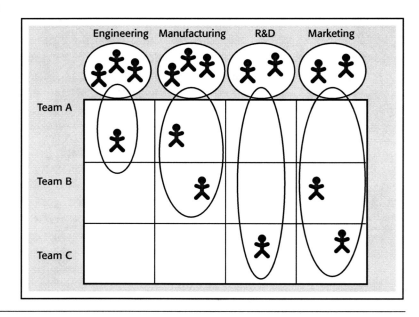

Chapter 1: Sorting Out the Puzzle Pieces

The cross-functional or matrix arrangement is able to pull together the people with the right skills onto the same team; but matrix organizations also present unique difficulties. Just because people are *assigned* to the same project team doesn't mean they *function* as a project team. The challenge of helping individuals coalesce as a team is no small feat.

The Cross-Work Puzzle

The project manager in a matrix situation faces a tough and classical dilemma: having clear responsibility with ambiguous authority. He or she is using borrowed people who still have ongoing responsibilities in their work unit and owe primary allegiance to their functional boss. Roles, responsibilities, and authorities are typically unclear in these settings. Who calls which shots? Because the functional boss does performance reviews, recommends raises, and makes future assignments, is it the functional boss whose work will generally get top priority when there's a conflict between project tasks and functional tasks?

Where organizations have created new work units from formerly cross-functional teams, authority is theoretically clearer, but work is hampered by the lack of attention to clarity in this new multiple marriage. Old discipline cultures (e.g., engineering and production) both enhance and inhibit work. These issues give rise to what I call the "cross-work puzzle." Solving that puzzle is critical to anyone in a project leadership position. I describe the puzzle as follows: how can the project manager overcome the confusion around roles, command the authority necessary, and put in place the key tools needed to get the job done?

This book grew out of my intensive experience at Addy and other organizations during the past couple of decades. The remaining chapters describe a practical approach for solving the cross-work puzzle.

Managing projects and introducing change using matrixed or cross-organizational teams involves weaving together the three elements mentioned earlier:

- **human interaction skills** which integrate the relationship elements with the technical and task components,
- **task component tools** which clarify objectives, schedules, authority and responsibilities,
- **whole-system health** which provides the substrate to nourish the effectiveness of work teams organization-wide.

This no-nonsense approach could be seen as "nonsense" by those who miss the point that success is dependent as much on the interactive human capabilities of project leaders as on the technical and work process components. **The human dimension, if neglected, always sabotages the technical.** It's a subtle point and not always easy to pull off, but in order for people to achieve cross-matrixed task force success, they have to blend the human interactive stages with task differentiation elements against a backdrop of system health.

The approach I am describing is practical. In skilled hands, the ideas here will lead to productive work. It clarifies roles in the otherwise ambiguous world of matrices. It works. Even more important, what I am describing is fulfilling to the human spirit.

Setting the Stage

Throughout this book I will use a series of vignettes to help illuminate the theory and clarify your understanding. Consider them as scenes from a movie or, even better, slices of real organizational life. To begin, let me introduce "Company Y," an international software firm with a head office in New York and various operations globally. We will pay particular attention to three employees there who are wrestling with cross-functional issues that are typical in large, complex organizations. We'll follow this trio through a series of thirteen scenes that occur during the project.

Jane is a 41-year-old manager. While she is brilliant in her technical field and very personable, she is inexperienced as a manager. Jane typifies what often happens when projects are managed by persons who are not clear about their own personal authority. They tend to lean towards one extreme of the authority continuum (dictatorship) or the other (consensus), and may even exercise a dictatorship while pretending consensus. As will be described further, such "leaders" are disruptive. The delays and mistrust they create cost organizations in lost revenue, lost opportunities, and market share.

Jane manages a young work force who feel strongly that all are equal and a manager is at her best when she is one of the gang. Many of them mistrust the use of authority and tend to (mistakenly) equate it with authoritarianism. While they may say that consensus doesn't work, they tend to move the organization towards consensus by their excessive concern for the feelings of others and their desire for equality in decision-making.

One of those in Jane's department is Eric, age 27. He is a widely-acknowledged technical whiz and a real star in programming the most esoteric computer languages. During the ensuing scenes you will hear him struggle with his new cross-functional assignment as he converses with his friend, Mary (age 35), a colleague who works with a different boss. Whereas Eric will seem to awaken to the need for clarity, Mary bounces back and forth and appears to have decided that "reality" demands a cautious non-risking state. She fails to see that there is no non-risk way to be in life or at work. She doesn't seem to understand that being cautious is itself a risk that may also lead to undesirable consequences.

SCENE I: The Assignment

Let's listen in as Eric and Mary walk down the corridor toward their work stations just after lunch.

Eric: "Well, his plots are not as complicated as John Le Carre's or as elegant as Graham Greene's, but trust me, it's a great read."

Mary: "Hey, I need a good read right now...Oh, Eric, you're being paged."

Eric turns and notices that the e-mail indicator light is flashing on his computer terminal. He types in his security code to receive his messages and the monitor beeps as his message comes on screen. Eric reads the communication and becomes slightly agitated.

Mary: "What's wrong?"

Eric: "I've been assigned to be a member on the Super-Jet project with forty other people. We are responsible for the fast-track launch of a new PIM—a Personal Information Manager, basically a calculator-sized computer. There's Rijib in New Delhi, and two cells of engineers, one in Zurich and another in London. Then, of course, there's the manufacturing division in Los Angeles and the marketing division across the street. There's no way we can make the schedule they want when people are so spread out. This is definitely a recipe for disaster. How irresponsible can they be?"

Eric is in a maze. Typically, members of such groups are frustrated by role confusion, by decision fuzziness, by the tug and pull between ongoing work and demands made on them by the new project, by schedule challenges. This situation is familiar to millions of employees and managers and may resonate with you.

There is a way out. The pages that follow spell out a formula for success in cross-work group tasks. While the formula alone may appear abstract, the text will highlight its practicality in day-to-day work. You'll see how the formula applies as you

Chapter 1: Sorting Out the Puzzle Pieces

follow Eric, with his boss Jane, and his friend Mary on their journey toward clarity in the vignettes.

SCENE II: THE CONFRONTATION

Eric is confronting Jane about her decision assigning him to the Super-Jet project.

Eric: "I still don't get why I have to be on this project!"

Jane: "Because you are perfect for it."

Eric: "Well, you could have asked me about it before you made your decision. I hope you don't mind me saying this, Jane, but that was a very unprofessional thing to do. And you know, cross-functional tasking in this building is tough enough without throwing a faceless bunch of collaborators from all over the world into the mix. Can't you see how complex this is going to be?"

Jane: "Eric, you shouldn't worry so much. We always manage to get through these projects. Besides, if it does become a maze I can't think of anyone better equipped to deal with that kind of complexity."

Though none of the characters in the drama know why, the project will probably be completed late, over budget, and with considerable burnout. Their situation is certainly made more difficult by the international networking. For most of us, the majority of task force work we do is at a single plant or site. When Titan 3 went into the wrong space orbit—a $500 million error—the *New York Times* reported, "Technicians at the Martin Marietta Corporation, who were in charge of the Titan 3 rocket's electrical system, mis-communicated with computer software engineers *in the same building.*"[4] Eric's concern about complexity certainly appears to be well-founded.

Three Components: A Formula for Success

In order to achieve success in organizations where work is carried out by cross-functional teams, *interactive human skills*, *task component clarity*, and *system health* must be in place and functioning.

Interactive human skills are those leadership skills necessary to manage a project where staying in touch and being clear about one's own needs are essential. I'll focus on these issues in Chapter 2.

Task component clarity obviously deals with how clear the team members are about the task. Confusion and lack of clarity are the norm in most projects and, unfortunately, are usually destructive. The most typical areas of confusion revolve around authority and decision-making issues. Few organizations, especially if they have grown rapidly, enjoy such clarity. And fast growth is a two-edged sword. While the revenue is welcome, trying to keep up with rampant growth allows little time to sort out organizational role issues. Companies whose product sells like hotcakes have generally paid little attention to the cross-functional issues critical for success. All their energy is spent hanging on during the accelerating rocketship ride. Then when the growth cycle has leveled off or starts to decrease, the problems show up. The task component section in Chapter 3 describes those critical factors.

System health is the medium that nurtures the other two. Effective human skills coupled with clear tasks are like a good seed planted in rich soil: with water and nurturance it will grow. On poor soil, perhaps after a quick promising start, it may be washed away. Poor interactive human skills, compounded with confusion about authority as well as other task components, are characteristics of unhealthy systems. The symptoms in this culture are quick-fixes, blaming, cover-ups, and other problems. System health will be described more fully in Chapter 4.

I have developed both a diagrammatic model (Figure 2) and a formula to represent the interdependence of these components. The formula is:

$$Project\ Success = (LISS + TC) \times SH$$

where LISS = the leader's interactive skill stage,

TC = the clarity about task components,

and SH = the system health of the organization.

In this formula, the first two components are additive and their effect is multiplied by the third element. Just as in a mathematical formula, the sum of the first two might be a significant number, but when multiplied by zero, the result is zero. In the organizational formula, poor system health will accelerate burnout in effective employees and will not sustain the processes necessary to successfully complete effective projects.

Figure 2
Three Components of Success

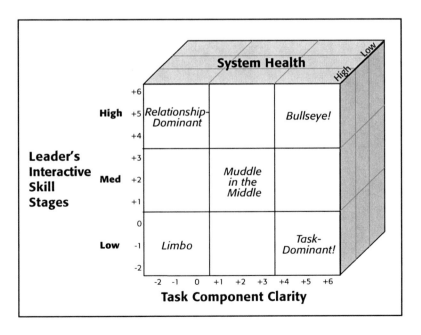

Chapter 2: Developing Effective Interaction Skills

"We don't see things as they are,

we see things as we are."

—ANAIS NIN

Interactive Skill Stages

Interactive skill stages describe the ability of the designated task force leader to effectively interact with people. The leader is the person given single-point accountability (SPA) by the organization. (I will describe SPA in Chapter 3.)

This leader must function at a high interactive developmental stage. Unfortunately, not all organizations pick as their SPA persons with excellent interactive capabilities. Because organizations that do this well are rare, I'm focusing first on the interactive developmental stage of the SPA leader. Without a leader who operates out of the higher stages of this scale, projects will flounder.

It is obvious that some persons interact in a much more effective way than others do. But measuring such development is, of course, elusive. To assist us I have created a scale that focuses on specific behavior. I suggest there are nine stages from -2 to +6, as illustrated in Figure 3.

This scale is based on the assumption that, **at the highest interactive skill stage, one is able to be open and honest, empathic towards others, and decisive.** The most effective leader has—and usually exudes—such skills.

Figure 3: Leader's Interactive Skill Scale[5]

	Stage	Description of Level	Inner Beliefs & Perceptions of Reality
High	+6	Empathic connection with others, yet still decisive	"I can walk in your moccasins and be myself which includes being decisive."
	+5	Is clear about wants	"I'll tell you what I need in order to succeed."
	+4	Acknowledgement of one's own part in the Interaction	"I help create the dance."
Medium	+3	Non-blaming; is specific about behavior and emotions	"Telling it straight is to give non-interpretive feedback."
	+2	Blaming, but is behaviorally specific	"Naming your behaviors proves my judgement."
	+1	Inner awareness, but manifest in blaming	"My judgements are the truth about you."
Low	0	Inner awareness, but non-communicative	"If I stay quiet, things will be 'cool.'"
	-1	Inner awareness, but outward distortion	"Telling the truth will make it worse."
	-2	Unaware, with 'cool' blaming	"Let reason conquer emotions."

This developmental scale reflects the degree to which one is increasingly self-aware and able to report it out with empathy and congruence. People are congruent when their words, tone, pace and gestures match. ("Thanks a lot!" with a sarcastic tone is an example of non-congruence.) Empathy refers to the capacity to "be in the other's shoes," to feel what the other is feeling without losing one's own separate and distinct experience or ability to decide.

You, the reader, will derive the most learning by allowing for the possibility that your behavior ranges among all nine stages. The more you allow this possibility—and become skilled in the higher interactive behaviors—the more you will choose the appropriate actions.

If I think of myself as only functioning at the higher stages (sainthood?) I will lose my capacity to be myself and to forgive others. While it may not be clear at first, please understand that the higher stages are not a matter of *technique* but rather of *being*. I will 'mess up' at times. The capacity to notice the 'mess up' (probably with help from friends) and get back on track is more important than always doing it right the first time—an impossible demand. "It's not what you do, it's what you do next."[6]

As people move from a -2 to a +6 stage, they "get it" that they create their own success or failure in their interaction with others and have the ability to be a distinctive self with clear but influenceable boundaries.

Note that the model consists of three major stages—low, medium and high—with three levels in each stage. **The purpose of this scale is not to dictate how one should act but, rather, how one can identify their own behaviors and predict consequences.**

Can you really teach old project leaders new tricks? Do adults have the ability to unlearn ways of interacting and being that feel "natural," but were really dysfunctional patterns learned as children which became habitual? The good news is that people can make a shift. Making that shift begins with awareness.

By the way, this model is not meant to cover clinically-deprived states known popularly by words such as sociopath or psychopath. These would score even lower. All of the stages in this formula are likely experienced by adequately functioning people. At times I may function at a -2, at times at a +6. I believe that most people hang out in the range from -2 to +1.

A. Stages of Distortion—Low Stages (-2, -1, and 0)

Leaders operating at the stages of distortion will strongly detract from the success of a project. Operating at these low stages is common in our culture because such interaction is familiar and "natural" to most people. Soap operas are mostly scripted within this bottom range. Many politicians operate here; blaming behavior is a common and expected strategy in election campaigns. Our litigious adversarial culture (with lawsuits and counter-suits) promotes low-level skills and pays handsome rewards to people who practice them well.

Perhaps it is necessary that competitors battle for market share using low-stage behavior, but this behavior within any given organization is destructive, stressful, demoralizing, and expensive. An open approach to dealing with differences found in the medium and high stages is much better than the conflict and avoidance behaviors in the low stages.

Unaware, with 'cool' blaming: -2

When people function at a -2 they are unaware of their own emotional state. On occasion, we all lapse into such a state or find our colleagues doing the same. Mary is obviously in such a state.

SCENE III: Playing the Blame Game

Mary is walking down the hallway. As she passes Eric's work station, she sees Eric, head in hands staring listlessly into his computer screen.

Mary: "Eric...Eric...are you all right?"

Eric: "Hello, Mary."

Mary: "Are you all right?"

Eric: "I feel rotten."

Mary: "You shouldn't be feeling anything, Eric. This is just work. You're taking all of this much too seriously. You don't see me bringing my feelings to the job, do you? Oh, you get your buttons pushed sometimes, but you just ignore the person or circumstances responsible and move on."

Eric: "I don't believe you, Mary. How are you able to turn out quality work when you're angry at management most of the time?"

Mary: *In a very measured voice* "I'm not angry, and as far as my attitude toward management goes, there's hardly a supervisor here who deserves respect. Take some advice, Eric. I hope you control your feelings because it just isn't safe to criticize around here."

Eric: "Sounds to me like you're playing the blame game, Mary."

Mary: *With emphasis* "Hey, a fact is a fact."

Unawareness is a state of separation from one's emotions, one's dogmatism, and insensitivity to others. Mary seems stuck in a dogmatism that blinds her to her out-of-touchness. She is **sure** she has no feeling. Too sure! Mary demonstrates how people at this stage are only too eager to tell others how they should feel, rather than being empathic with them and learning how the other person actually does feel.

People at the -2 stage believe that reason should always triumph over emotion and that emotionality is weakness. Mary distances herself from her emotions by blaming when she says "...there's hardly a supervisor here who deserves respect." She thinks she's stated a fact given her 'cool,' computer-like tone. She has simply denied the emotional, feeling part of her being.

Those who accept the possibility that they may be unaware at times are more likely to respond when asked, "How do you feel?" with an open stance, "I'm not aware of what I'm feeling now."

Inner Awareness, but Outward Distortion: -1

When people function at a -1, they are aware but choose to distort. Granted there are situations where distorting the truth may seem wise, or even necessary, but if a leader consistently functions at a stage -1 or -2, the system will develop reinforcing links where distorting the truth becomes the standard way of behavior. For instance, people will make promises for delivery that they never intend to meet and that the other doesn't really believe. Or they might send double messages by joking when they are serious.

Self-distortion is subtle. Ironically, few humans ever see themselves as dishonest, but observe enough of that behavior in others to conclude that the stance is widespread. Often such distortion is really an unaware -2 rather than a deliberate lie, but the observer can only guess. Since each of us tends to know our own intentions as honest, it is difficult to imagine that whomever we are conversing with may be judging that we are shading the truth. This appears to be a behavior that is easy to see in others but difficult to detect in ourselves.

Perhaps the best way to tell which stage you (or others) are at is to carefully listen to the language being used. At the -1 stage, one is deliberately stating the opposite of whatever he or she is thinking or feeling. In all stages through +2 the belief system is manifested by victim language such as "You pushed my button." Only at the +3 stage does one begin to realize that "I push my own buttons." This is seen as a radical and absurd notion at these lower stages.

Practically speaking, "leaders" functioning at a -2, -1, or 0 will be dysfunctional. These "crazy-makers" confuse and bewilder others and their behavior will stifle team effectiveness. The main casualty here will be the project itself, which is likely to fail or at least be significantly delayed.

Inner Awareness, but Non-Communicative: **0**

You see these persons all the time. They are the quiet ones who hold back and communicate little, if at all. Non-communicators present themselves as a huge blank screen on which their colleagues project whatever they imagine about the non-communicators. The non-communicator's intentions are a mystery. They may have the very best intent, but their absence of communication initiative creates a vacuum. Like the famous *Rorschach Ink Blot Test*, the vacuum gets filled with the projected hopes and fears of others. Interaction is minimal or one-sided with information flowing to the non-communicator. People guess what the non-communicator wants—and usually miss.

Let's return for a minute to the formula (LISS + TC) x SH = Project Success. From a mathematical perspective, a LISS score of 0 will add nothing to the success of the project, but negative scores will have a significant impact on the outcome—even when overall system health is high.

If you catch yourself in any of these three dysfunctional stages, don't despair. In fact, congratulations for having noticed! The key to moving to the medium stages is awareness.

B. Stages of Awakening — Medium Stages (+1, +2, +3)

Inner Awareness, But Manifest in Blaming: +1

Contrasted to computer-like blaming of the cool -2, this is hot stuff. The intensity is rising. In fact, some people venture here only to later retreat to a lower stage because of unpleasant consequences. The dilemma here is that while this blaming is revealing—rather than hidden in the pretend logic of the -2 stage—both the sender and the receiver may be confused about what is being revealed. We witnessed this behavior in the vignettes:

> Scene I   "How irresponsible." (Eric)
> Scene II "That was unprofessional." (Eric)
> Scene III "It isn't safe to criticize around here." (Mary)

If Eric and Mary believe that these statements are reality about the others rather than their own judgments about the situation, then they are in a state of distortion. Jane would also be distorting if she swallows these judgments as facts about herself.

SCENE IV: CURRENT BEHAVIOR REVEALS CHILDHOOD PATTERNS

Jane is walking down the hall on her way to a meeting. She meets Mary coming back from her mid-afternoon break. They stop briefly and make small talk. Jane continues down the hall to her meeting, and something catches her eye as she passes Eric's work station. An obviously troubled Eric is staring into his monitor aimlessly. She stops.

Jane: "Are you okay, Eric?" *Eric turns in his chair to face her.*

Eric: "I told you this project would be a disaster. *Pointing to the screen.* What a mess. We're already experiencing delays and everybody's playing the blame game. I haven't met anyone yet who is willing to take responsibility for their actions. Hell, I've even begun to point the finger myself. It sort of reminds me of growing up."

Jane: "What do you mean?"

Eric: "I had five brothers and two sisters. In my family, we were experts at the blame game. Since I was the middle child, I was always trying to please everyone and fix everything. I was the peacemaker. This project is driving me nuts, Jane. I'm stuck in the middle, just like when I was a kid, and there's nowhere to go for answers. It's like trying to negotiate a peace treaty between factions that refuse to compromise. Upper management has really screwed up by not providing the leadership necessary to end these turf wars, but the worst thing of all is that nobody seems to care about the company."

Eric is trapped in an old pattern. While beginning to see that he may be repeating family history, he also seems stuck on blaming. Eric is able to name the blame game, but keeps on placing the problem outside of himself. He sees himself as a helpless, powerless victim. He falsely believes that only others can create positive change. He's repeating his family story as if he's a victim permanently trapped in the past. Eric doesn't realize that he is co-creating his own present. Blindly locked into an old pattern, Eric is acting helpless with no perceived power to change the current pattern.

Two things are clear from Eric's statements in Scenes I and II above. First as the sender of these accusations, Eric interprets a particular behavior with the words "irresponsible and unprofessional." This signals that these traits were likely a major theme in Eric's growing up. The other revelation is that Eric is unhappy with Jane. These are neither objective facts nor devoid of emotionality! This is not to say that Jane's behavior is desirable or that she plays no part in the interaction. Nor is it to say that Eric should not have interpretations (which are simply a form of judgments), because everybody has interpretations.

Rather, at a higher interactive skill stage, one knows that one's interpretations are exactly that, *interpretations,* and not facts about the other. That Jane selected Eric and communicated by e-mail may be a fact. But the interpretations by Eric about the behavior reveals **his** lens for viewing life situations of this kind. Eric may have called the e-mail notification "unprofessional" while another employee might have interpreted the same behavior as a reward—a statement about their being special. It's in the eye of the beholder.

Mary's statement from Scene III is more subtle. In her first three words, "It isn't safe," she has externalized her experience, as she also does in her statements from Scenes I and II. She too is probably reflecting a view from her childhood world. She will not see this clearly unless she moves higher on the scale and understands that there isn't an "it" but rather an "I" responding internally to some external event. Only then will she acknowledge that "I feel safe or unsafe," while someone at her side may feel the opposite. "It" is her projected reality.

When operating at +1 we place our locus of control externally. "You pushed my button" is still the theme. It's your fault. I'm the victim. The positive step in +1 is that the person is emoting, even though it is in a blaming way.

If the receiver is able to function at a +4 or higher, perhaps the interaction will be successful because of the receiver's ability to change an interaction from reactivity to dialogue. Otherwise, the interaction will either escalate into a more intense conflict or lead to a "cutoff," an abrupt end of the conversation and perhaps any future attempt at conversation.

The dominant mode of communication is +1 among many who say that they "tell it straight." That is, they 'blame' well—usually to a third person about the person they are blaming. A +1 communication is full of arguing, blaming, and confusing judgments as "facts." If you want to see +1 (and lower) stages at its best, watch soap operas. Unfortunately, these learned styles are seen as the **natural** way people talk.

Systems thinker Peter Senge distinguishes discussion from dialogue, noting that the literal meaning of discussion is to "heave ideas at each other."[7] Percussion, concussion, and discussion come from the same root word. Discussion is adversarial. Dialogue (from the Greek *dia logos* ; literally "through the word") requires both a commitment to explore meanings and a higher skill level of interaction. You won't find much real dialogue at these medium stages. The interactive skills for dialogue await the higher stages of +4, +5, and +6.

Blaming, But is Behaviorally Specific: +2

This is a transitional stage where the speaker is able to describe a situation. The stage of +2 is transitional between a victim state where control of self is outside oneself ("You pushed my button"), and a self-responsible state where people begin to understand their part in the interactive dance ("I push my own buttons"). In +1, the statement is "How irresponsible," as if it's an imbedded trait. But in + 2, the speaker is at least able to refer to the specific event ("You communicated by e-mail") even though still holding the judgment.

Stating the judgment still tends to escalate the conflict at this +2 stage since the accused rarely agrees with the judgment of the accuser. If the presenting event is described, agreement or verification of the behavior by the accused is often easily obtained; but the accused is rarely inclined to agree with the accusation. Also at this stage, the accuser will likely believe that the process of enumerating the specifics simply **proves** his or her judgment.

However, adding specificity does give the parties to the interaction an opening to move from the morass created by the blaming of +1. Individuals stuck at a +2 stage have not yet arrived at a self-responsible place although the seeds have been planted by the new ability to specify the precipitating event. That descriptive capacity can assist the breakthrough to +3. But at level two, people will still confuse judgments with facts, which clouds their ability to be specific. The false belief will persist that these language distinctions are simply semantics.

As one moves beyond the +1 level, a slow evolutionary shift begins to happen The person begins to suspect that they cannot **know** reality—that their reality isn't necessarily **the** reality. This is the beginning of the capacity for empathic listening i.e., "Your perception is important to me— not to argue with, but to build with!"

In the following scene, Eric is continuing to reach for his own power. Eric's boss, Jane, is assisting in his growth by listening and owning her own pain.

SCENE V: THE FLASH OF SELF-INSIGHT

We see Eric approaching Jane's office. Jane is seated at her desk and is on the phone. Eric gently knocks on the door. Jane, still engaged in conversation, motions for him to take a seat.

Jane: *Into the phone* "Okay, Joe … let me get back to you on that … yeah … This afternoon. … Okay … Take care … Just relax." *She hangs up.* "Hi, Eric. What can I do for you?"

Eric: *He leans forward and says, in a loud, intense voice* "Jane, I'm having a lot of difficulty with this project. I'm in a fog. I just don't understand what it is that you expect from me. This thing has turned into an absolute nightmare. I'm so sick of the blaming and the fingerpointing that's already going on that I'm just about ready to hang it up."

Jane: "I had no idea that you were this upset. I don't know what to say. Maybe you're looking for the answers in the wrong places. Maybe you're counting too much on others to resolve things.

Eric: "Could be.... I'm beginning to see that I often act like a victim without even realizing it. I keep expecting someone else to give me the answers, to make it easier, you know, to fix it for me. It never seems to work, and I'm always left with this frustrated feeling."

Jane: "Painful, isn't it? You're saying a lot about how I often feel about myself."

Eric: "You? Oh, come on. You radiate self confidence. I've never seen you in a quandary like this."

Jane: "You may have never seen it, but it's often true. I wish I felt more confident about myself. Look, Eric, sounds like both of us have a higher regard for the other than we do for ourselves! I think you're doing fine."

Eric: "Maybe you're right, but I feel stumped right now. Maybe, I'm waiting for answers instead of taking my own initiative, but I still can't talk about this project without blaming someone else. Boy, I hope I don't sound as helpless to you as I sound to myself sometimes."

Jane: "Hang in, Eric."

Eric has begun to become aware of the ways his habitual patterns confound, confuse, and complicate his life.

Non-Blaming; is Specific About Behavior and Emotion: +3

The awakening of the higher interactive skill stages accelerates as people develop their capacity to be both specific about the presenting events and specific about the emotional impact on themselves. "I don't like it that you notified me by e-mail" is an example of such specificity.

The crucial skill to be learned here goes far beyond choosing the correct language. The ability to practice this +3 skill "beyond technique" comes only when one no longer believes that one's judgment about a particular event is a fact, but rather a judgment (although perhaps, an appropriate one). Accompanying that insight comes the realization that there are other ways to perceive and judge the same event. There is no denial intended here about the importance of judgments. Rather the separation is now easily made between observable behavior, possible interpretations, and possible emotions.

Observable behavior

Eric leaned forward and said in a loud voice, "Jane, I'm having a lot of difficulty with this project!"

Possible interpretations by Jane

- Eric is being pushy.
- Eric is concerned about the company's success.
- Eric has a lot at stake.
- Eric is afraid.
- Eric thinks that background noise is making it difficult for Jane to hear.

Possible emotions depending on Jane's interpretation

- Jane felt irritated (at 'pushy' Eric).
- Jane felt appreciative (towards a 'concerned' Eric).
- Jane felt empathic (towards Eric and his 'stake').
- Jane felt drawn towards and wanted to help (a 'frightened' Eric).
- Jane felt overwhelmed (by a 'loud' Eric).

Here's an obvious but often forgotten principle of human behavior: one's emotions are in response **not** to the event itself, but to one's interpretation of the event.

This flies directly in the face of the popular mental model that "I know you by your actions." Not so, rather "I know you by my interpretation of your actions." People create those interpretations in the millisecond between the event and their own emotional response.

Do you realize the significance of this? Understanding this distinction is a radically new paradigm for most humans. That singular insight can move me from a world where I believe others **cause** me to think or feel certain things, to a world where I profoundly realize that I create my interpretations and therefore am responsible for my own thoughts and feelings. Other people do not "make me" feel/think. I "make me." Truly grasping this frees me to choose to evolve from **reactivity**, which characterizes the animal world and most of the human evolution up to this point, to **creativity** where I empower myself to see **me** as the primary creator of my life.

So **my** choice of the above interpretations will evoke different emotional impacts in me. Choice here is tricky, because one part of me is **reacting** with interpretations imbedded in my early years in that first growing-up environment, while a developing part of me is aware of these reactions and is examining them. I may notice that my emotional intensity greatly exceeds the stimulus of the moment and therefore is likely related to unfinished growing-up issues. I may notice that I, by my interpretation, have apparently triggered myself into an emotional state that is oh-so-familiar to similar states experienced in my early years.

Phrases like "My button was pushed" or " I was triggered" are colloquial ways that victims express this reactivity. By contrast, non-victims recognize that "I pushed my own button" or "I pulled my own trigger."

At the +3 level I am beginning to "get it" that nobody else pushes my button. Nobody else makes me feel a certain way. I am choosing my behaviors and how I react to the behavior of others. They are not somebody else's fault . . . not my parents. . . not the work colleague I am dealing with today. The locus of control is within me. This becomes manifest in my ability to state clearly how I am affected by your specific behavior. I also now recognize many possible emotional responses to the same stimulus: "You notified me by e-mail."

I liked...

I disliked...

I'm troubled...

I'm pleased...

Now at +3, I'm 'telling it straight' without blaming. I notice my judgments and realize they are situational and uniquely personal. I also honor that facts are distorted by perception and decisions in life are made based on one's best judgment. In such a +3 moment, I can say "Here I choose to take my stand, and, of course, I may regret this."

C. Stages of Responsibility and Connection— High Stages (+4, +5, +6)

Acknowledgment of One's Own Part in the Interaction: +4

Now we move to the higher skill stages. Notice that the higher the skill stage, the more difficult it is to fake or script the skill. The following stages are about being who you really are in a personally and socially responsible way. These are not techniques.

> *Fundamentally, the higher stages are based on a belief system, not techniques of communication.*

People operating at +4 see their own responsibility in the presenting dilemma and can break through the "stuckness" experienced at lower stages. Recall that in Scene III Mary said "It's not safe to criticize around here." This is +1 blame. At +2 level, the statement may be, "It's not safe to criticize because I tried and a manager told me, 'You should change your attitude.'"

Assuming that, indeed, a manager had made this statement, then the speaker has added a specific, a quote. In the reported interchange, the speaker and receiver (manager) traded +1 accusations: "It's not safe to criticize around here" and "You should change your attitude." If neither person has the capacity to rise above the +1 stage, then each reinforces the other and the conflict is escalated or they cut off from each other through attack, denial of the problem, acquiescing, or leaving.

Figure 4
Mutually
Destructive and
Reinforcing
Communication
Loops

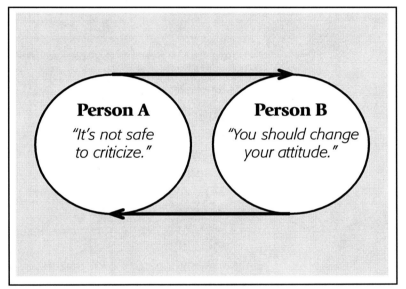

At the +3 level, either party can break the pattern by refusing to continue blaming and instead owning their own emotional state. Either party can say "Wait. I'm troubled by what I just said and by your response."

Will this break the escalating cycle? Perhaps, perhaps not. There is no guarantee that responses at a higher skill stage will produce desired results. They certainly encourage higher functioning by others, but their deepest benefit is for the person speaking. By maintaining the higher stages I, the speaker, will begin to experience more clarity for myself about myself. I'm beginning to separate what's in me from what's outside me.

With a +4 response, the speaker's ownership is added, Person A might have said "I don't feel safe if I think I'm being criticized. It's always been tough for me to share what bothers me."

This is not to say that people need always share this personal part of themselves. There are no "shoulds" here. I am describing capacities rather than techniques. Having the capacity to own one's tendency can, at times, be useful. Ownership also means acknowledging a mistake I made, or a remark I regret, or an action that could easily have been misunderstood.

Levels +3 and +4 often go together. At the +4 level, results are additive in that the speaker owns that she is at least a co-creator of the perceived situation. The behavior at +4 enables the sender to fully explore his part in the dance. The beliefs at this level are:

- I push my own buttons.
- I project onto others my greatest criticisms about myself.
- It takes two to tango and I help create the dance.
- My early growing up experiences affect my current life.
- I am responsible for my choices.
- The locus is within me.
- I want to separate out what I bring to the party from what others bring.

Acknowledging one's own part in the interaction is not an act of self-blame. The +4 level is not the opposite of +1 where "it's all somebody else's fault" and now at +4 "It's all my fault." At this level people own their possible part in the dilemma without getting bogged down in self-blaming. Rather, they are open learners refusing to give away their personal power and looking for ways to create the circumstances of their life. (Even though it is understood that life is lived in the midst of dysfunctional systems where individuals cannot create certain external forces.)

SCENE VI: The Change in Stance

Jane and Eric are seated in the employee lounge talking about Eric's day off.

Eric: "I can't thank you enough for giving me that extra day off. It's made all the difference in the world. I had the time to confront what was really bothering me. I realize that there aren't any permanent solutions for anything."

Jane: "I surely agree. Lately, everything about this place reeks of chaos and indecision."

Eric: "You, too, huh?"

Jane: "Sure ... does that bother you?"

Eric: "Yes and no. Really, I'm pretty excited. You see, Jane, I've spent a lot of years letting other people shape my attitudes and make my decisions for me. And I've been repeating that same pattern on this project. I've always had the talent to function on my own, but I don't take the initiative. Look, you know my skill level. I'm one of the best employees in this company. I don't want to bicker and fight with co-workers over minor details. I want to communicate so I can do my job."

Jane: "I really like what you're saying, Eric. As a manager I've experienced something similar—only in reverse."

Eric: "Come on."

Jane: "It's true. I'm just now beginning to realize that I don't have to pretend to have all of the answers. What a relief. It sounds like we're entering the twenty-first century, Eric."

Eric: "What?"

Jane: "Oh, I'm just thinking about some of the current organizational ideas. You know, things like constant change, unpredictability, dialogue—the need for it, and systems thinking. Like, what's systemic and how can I be proactive in a positive way to change what I think isn't working?"

Is Clear About Wants: +5

Level +5 is one of illuminated clarity about your wants. Until one practices the abilities described in the previous two levels, wants will be distorted by an inability to distinguish between facts and interpretations, and between what is my want and your need. The statement "I'm doing this for your own good!" illustrates the latter distortion.

The hallmark of the +5 level is a clear sense of self-needs, strengths, and shortcomings. Without these, one can remain mired in belief systems that prevent knowing—let alone asking for—what one wants. Some typical dysfunctional beliefs that often accompany the lower levels:

- Stating wants is selfish or pushy.
- Asking assumes getting.
- It's childish to ask.
- Others should know what I want.
- Asking sets me up for painful rejection.
- Stating wants puts unfair pressure on others.
- Stating wants equals demanding.

In contrast, some functional beliefs practiced at the +5 level:

- It is important that I clearly ask for what I want.
- Other people are responsible for their own emotional reactions to my requests.
- Other people can't read my mind—I need to be clear.
- I have the skills to ask effectively.
- Success is directly related to my ability to get what I need in order to do my job well.

People with self-clarity send and receive wants primarily as statements, rather than as demands, but are willing to "go to bat" for what they think is crucial. When in command, they are willing to make unpopular decisions to achieve goals and indeed to make demands when necessary. Those unable to do so contribute to poor team functioning and cross-group friction. One reason so called "difficult" employees or "resistant" co-workers behave that way is because they rarely know what is specifically expected of them, i.e., what their colleagues or bosses want. Often vague, interpretive words are bandied about instead of clear wants. Person B, for instance, wants more professionalism, initiative, or cooperation from Person C. Since each of these words means different behaviors to different people, such words actually contribute to creating conflict.

At each successive level there is a growth in the capacity to hear the other. As my boundaries get clear, I feel less threatened about hearing others' feelings and wants and more empathic towards them.

At +5 the leader manifests the cumulative levels of +3, +4, and +5. Here are examples that are additive to a +1 demand to "Cooperate more."

+3 "I'm troubled that you've missed the last two due dates for your computer response to Project A."

+4 "I can see that my verbal request style without a follow-up written message contributed to the confusion."

+5 "I want your response by 3:00 PM US West Coast time each Thursday to the questions on page 8 in the Project A Manual."

To be in a + 5 stage is to know myself, what I value, what's important to me, what is important to others, what my goal is and, therefore, what I want. From this stance, I can hear a "no" as "no to my request" rather than as a personal rejection by the other. An individual at the +5 stage risks stating specific wants, e.g., "I want you (my boss) to support the following initiatives and budget requests. I need these to do my job well." My wants come from my internal experience and are felt as well as thought. Receivers will likely receive these wants of mine as spontaneous and congruent with what they are noticing in my tone, face, and gestures. And if it is truly what **I** want, I will state that and not hide behind the collective "**we want.**"

Here's an important distinction: these wants should reflect what the individual needs to achieve project success rather than personal desire. The effective leader's point of reference is always the project and what project success requires.

Empathic Connection with Others, yet Still Decisive: +6

The capability to live one's life at a +6 belongs to all, but no one achieves that capability all the time. While humans have the capacity to live at various stages, it is not possible, until one has experienced a stage, to fully understand that stage.

The goal of this highest interactive stage is to be clear about one's self while staying connected to others. For the self to stay clear in the midst of resistance, hostility, sabotage, or ambiguity and still maintain rapport is exceedingly difficult. Of course no one can stay connected in all circumstances, especially when dealing with someone whose life pattern is stuck at stages -2, -1, 0, and +1.

The leader's stage sets the stage.

Imagine you are leading a meeting whose members are performing at various stages:

Leader (+6)

Member A (+4)	Member D (+1)
Member B (0)	Member E (+6)
Member C (+2)	Member F (-2)

In situations like this, the hypothesis is:

The stage at which the leader functions will influence the stage of the members.

It's hard for members to function at a stage higher than the leader. If the leader functions at +4 to +6, then all others have the possibility of improving. However, without training in the interactive skill stages, I would not expect Member F to exceed a +1.[8] Also, while Member B may surprise all when she starts talking, I would not expect she would reach the highest stages. Likewise, Member D.

The more developed the leader, the less she will get "stuck" in extended arguments or explanations with the least developed members. The second dimension (task components) will underscore the system authority needed by the SPA (single-point accountability) leader. Also, if the SPA leader is attempting to lead in an unhealthy system (the third dimension of this book), then the task forces and meetings are likely influenced by people at lower levels on the scale. Since this is an unaware process (in an unhealthy system) the influence is operating on a covert rather than an overt level. The (usually) unintentional sabotage will be manifest by:

- attempts to get decisions reversed,
- seemingly "rational" explanations going on and on (disguised arguing),
- "heaving" ideas, blaming,
- the real talk happening outside of meetings.

The +6 leader will not be drawn from the course that has been set by the above messages. The art here is to remain flexible enough to ferret out important data that may be hidden in resistant communication and still "stay the course." A response to a persistent effort to get the decision reversed by one person might be

> *"Joe, I understand that you think my decision is unwise. You've been consistent with that position. No one can accuse you of being wishy-washy about that. Thanks for your input, but my decision will stick and I need your ideas to make it work." At this point the leader looks elsewhere in the room and says, "Are there any comments about other aspects of the work?"*

OR

> *"I'm not willing to discuss this further in this meeting but I'd be pleased to meet with you afterwards in meeting Room A."*

If the blaming is coming from many different people, the +6 leader might say

> *"Well it looks like you have enough people to form a Blame-the-Leader club. If you decide to meet after work I'll even be willing to meet with you as long as you pay for my drink...but for now I'm going to take the next steps on this task. So here's what I want you to do."*

Effective leaders use a tone and demeanor that comes from a **light** rather than a **heavy** place. In the "blame-the-leader club" quote above, the impact would be quite different if it were gruffly stated with a scowl. That would make it come across as sarcasm. But when delivered with playfulness and a smile, it's perceived instead as "having fun with" or "joking together." The leader will only come from a "light" place if he is genuinely clear about his direction and "centered" in the midst of the conflict.

If the leader has confronted the resistance (blaming, etc.) by "swallowing it whole," he will likely feel intense, perhaps angry and defensive, and slip into +1 behavior. He will feel heavy rather than light. Then the response will likely be sarcastic (as apparent in the tone) rather than light. A leader operating at the higher interactive stages and feeling angry and defensive might acknowledge her heaviness and defensiveness and re-spond–not with sarcasm–by saying

> *"Look I'm very upset at what I've been hearing. I don't like being blamed. I also don't want to spend time defending myself or the decision that was made. I believe a further discussion will not lead to clarity because I believe all of us are clear, but some are simply opposed.*

I honor that. So be it. We did not reach a consensus in the agreed time so a decision has been made. Now I'm going to take the lead in what I think is next. So here's what's next...."

No script can be written for +6. At this stage the leader is exhibiting his or her personal authority in balance with a connectedness with others. "Ideally, what (the leader) chooses to do or to be is the thing that seems most likely to be useful in the moment and in the given situation. This is situational..."[9]

When a leader is functioning with +6 behavior, she is empathic and able to enter the context of another. In a session where members were deeply conflicted, the leader invited each to tell their story in the context of the task at hand, while others were to inquire and empathize. A team member disclosed

"When I was assigned to this project, I was excited because I believed this could be of significance to our company . . . Now, I feel pressured to protect (certain aspects of the product) and think that some of you are withholding important information."

Leader: "Imagine that this is a classical drama and that some here are assigned to be your antagonists. Who would they be?"

Member: "Joe and Sarah. And so I've developed my own *intelligence unit* to get information I think you're withholding."

Leader: "Oh, how wonderful. I love spy stories. Do others?"

Members: "Yes."

Leader: "Are you willing to risk exposing this spy operation?"

Member: "Sure, because for one thing, it isn't working!"
Group Laughter.

Leaders operating at +6 are masters of feedback and empathy. They have the capacity to engage in feedback, not as a one-way street, but as mutual exploration. This transcends the typical negative association of feedback as a one-way tearing down of the person. Furthermore, feedback at this higher stage is reciprocal, sought and valued, but not used as a definition of one's self.[10] That is, I honor feedback from you as a glimpse into your experience and perception, your "reality." Indeed, I value and consider your words while remaining a separate self and continue to make my decisions about my life. I avoid the extremes of ignoring your feedback or swallowing it whole. Such feedback is a growing, learning, imaginative process where possibilities for an even greater interaction and greater productivity emerge.

Empathy is the capacity to know another human and is the foundation of dialogue and reciprocal feedback. When functioning at a low skill stage, the fear associated with empathy is the loss of self. If I listen to you I may lose me! Only the individual functioning at the higher stages can empathize because she knows that she is a separate self who will not get sucked into or lose her self in the other, yet will acknowledge any fears that exist.

Empathy and clarity about self are twins. I can only get into the skin of the other if I have my own skin self-defined and know my own boundaries. This means being clear about my personal authority. Only then am I capable of giving and receiving behaviorally specific feedback. Only then can I function at a higher skill capability with full understanding that such engagement is in the interest of both parties. I am no longer listening just because good leaders listen, but because I profoundly sense that both my relationship to the other and my knowledge about myself is enhanced by the interaction. This kind of interaction creates energy in both parties. Both finish the interaction feeling stronger. It's win-win. Contrast that with win-lose interactions where one party walks away feeling stronger and the other weaker.

Weber and Levine have written, "The ancient concept of 'hospitality' is helpful... The 'host' and 'hostess' in other cultures were hospitable partly in what was given to the guest, but also in what was received from the guest or stranger... It is interesting to note that 'guest' and 'host' were once the same word, as were also 'give' and 'receive'. A spirit of mystery and imagination is cultivated where what is to be discovered is greater than the sum of the parts and is co-created in a joint venture." [11]

At higher skill levels a leader understands this reciprocal nature of interaction and of the mutuality of power. Empowerment programs in organizations often fail because the following mental model is operating: "Those with power (top management) are giving power to those who had no power."[12] Nonsense. All have power. The issue is rather how power is used. Apathy is a use of power, as is sabotage.

Leaders operating at the higher stages are free to create an empathic/listening environment, a climate for hospitality, a learning organization precisely because they are clear about self and clear about their own authority. They do not create a Pollyanna world of consensus, of egalitarianism, but rather one where meanings are deeply explored and, paradoxically, decisiveness is valued. Interacting at the top of the scale makes possible the creation of a learning way of life—a learning organization.[13]

The leader who is clear about self and what he wants, willing to be decisive and hold people accountable, speaks with "I" messages, maintains a non-anxious presence, and empathically tunes into others is positioned to untangle the dilemma of cross-group work.[14]

But functioning at such a high stage is not enough. To solve the cross-work puzzle, this behavior must also be accompanied by the capacity to help clarify task components.

Chapter 3: Making Task Components Clear

> *"Without clarity about authority and*
> *continuous maintenance of work role*
> *relationships....projects will fail no matter*
> *how brilliantly they were structured."*
>
> —ROBERT P. CROSBY

People skills, of course, are not enough. The project leader also needs a set of skills for carrying out projects. This chapter presents a scale of critical task components. I offer this graded scale based on decades of experience guiding both successful and failed project groups.15 Whether the stages described here build sequentially in importance as indicated on my scale or whether the higher stages are simply a list of equal requisites is open to question and research.

Like the Leader's Interactive Skill scale in the previous chapter, this Task Components scale also consists of nine different stages grouped into three groups of low, medium and high effectiveness as illustrated in Figure 5.

Depicted at the +1 point on the scale and upwards are the critical components necessary to both implement and sustain successful cross-functional work. This scale is meant to enhance the standard project management planning and control tools rather than replace them. My emphasis here is on those factors I have most often found missing, even as I have consulted with full-time project managers well-schooled in the practices of project management.

A. Low Task Stages (-2, -1, 0)

Desperate Heroic Efforts: -2

Those at the -2 stage think that management can't manage and tasks get completed only by heroic efforts. This is "how things get done" and they are convinced there is no other way. So the -2 people who get put in charge of projects are those who thrive on heroic efforts. They have learned how to manipulate in a crisis and believe they must "rescue" projects from inept management and impotent systems. They cajole, persuade, and do whatever it takes on the assumption that managers can't manage and that they, and they alone, can save the project.

Figure 5 Task Components Scale

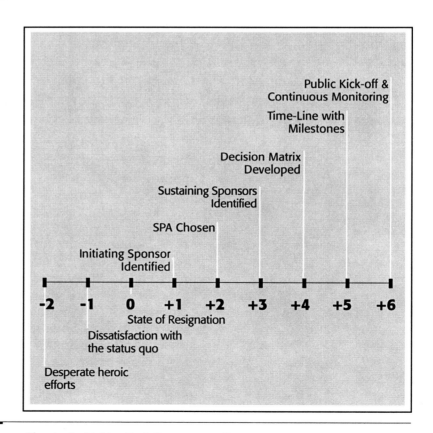

Chapter 3: Making Task Components Clear

Because such **hero** behavior is learned in the earliest growing-up environment, people fulfilling those roles are **not** likely to support change. They are neither prepared to function in a different way nor to focus on making the system work. They believe the system sucks .... always has and always will.

But such behavior causes a vicious cycle: a cynical view of management coupled with the (non) system in place to achieve success in cross-functional work feeds a blaming, personal style. Companies trapped in this behavior cycle cannot have consistently successful projects.

Figure 6 Result of Heroic Effort

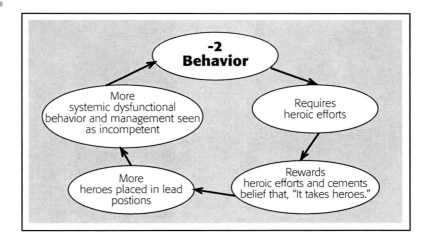

Dissatisfaction with the Status Quo: *-1*

Little changes when the stage moves to a -1. This represents an awareness that things could be better. This awareness, however, is usually accompanied by more blaming because things aren't any better. At the -1 stage there is no competence to effect a change. The pressure is on to achieve results, but the leader does not know how to successfully manage the matrix, even though that person may have read numerous books about what to do and attended trainings in project management. Left with little guidance and even less task clarity, the leader's frantic self-exhortation is to "just do something." Blaming top management or other departments is also a favorite theme. There is a clear correlation between the low stages of this task components scale and a similar position on the interactive skills scale.

State of Resignation: *0*

"We've tried everything. There's no way to change things around here. Might as well give up."

This state of resignation is slightly more positive than -1, but only if the organization isn't <u>stuck</u> here. In -1, there is active blaming and trying; in 0, there is only despair. Ironically, organizations in despair may feel the pain enough to seek help. Despair, **as a stage**, is more positive if acknowledged than the frantic trying that often comes at the -1 and -2 stages. It doesn't often happen, but despair can galvanize the organization and muster enough energy to move the members into action.

B. Medium Functioning Levels (+1, +2, +3)

Initiating Sponsor Identified: *+1*

It seems obvious that authority issues need to be addressed early in projects, but because it's not comfortable for people to do this, they are often avoided. As a result ,many people operate without clear understanding and agreement about the role of authority in organizations.

Authority *per se* is neither bad nor good. Rather, authority is vital because decisions of all types—resource, technical, scheduling and others—must consistently be made. The wise use of authority is the necessary glue that holds project teams together. Denying its necessity is disastrous because authority always emerges, either deliberately or by default. (Read *Lord of the Flies* to see the perils of authority by default.)

So-called self-managing teams have particular difficulty handling authority issues because of a dangerous belief that "we all have the same authority." Management books written about self-managed teams either lightly touch on or ignore issues of authority altogether. But not dealing with it causes results like those which Volvo experienced at their Uddevalla Plant in Sweden which attempted self-management teams and eventually was closed. As written in my earlier management book,

> *"The jargon* self-management teams *is popular today. Unfortunately, many employees and managers define such teams without taking into account the need for clear management authority. It is our experience that teams will fail without the **balance** we describe. The tension in political democracy between freedom and justice, and between citizen influence and government authority, will be with us forever. Likewise, the struggle in organizations about how to tap the energy and expertise of employees, while also managing with optimum authority, is an ongoing one."*[16]

That balance—the crucial ability to find the right combination of management authority and employee influence—apparently eluded the Volvo executives.

> *"It takes 50 hours of labor to build a car at Uddevalla. In contrast, the time required to build a car in Japan is 17 hours and in the United States, 25 hours. The Uddevalla plant workers take longer to assemble a car than the workers at the other three more traditional Volvo plants. 'The approach, which entailed slashing layers of management and eliminating all foremen ... (also aimed to) give them (employees) more control over their jobs.' I would rather have retrained the foremen and groups to achieve the balance emphasized in this book."*[17]

In 1994, an influential observer of Sweden's automobile manufacturing industry offered another similar insight:

"When, for example, Uddevalla's autonomous teams and holistic job design were supported by a participative and hard-driving management, *the result was accelerated and simultaneous advances in productivity, quality, and market responsiveness. The plant was close to a real breakthrough when top management decided to lay it idle for capacity reasons."* (Emphasis added.) [18]

Levels of Authority

Two levels of sponsorship are especially relevant in projects— the sustaining and initiating sponsors. The task members' immediate supervisors are the **sustaining sponsors**. The job of the sustaining sponsors is to support and assist their subordinates who are task group members. The cross-functional task team as a whole is sponsored by the individual who is the common boss of all personnel on the task force. This is the **initiating sponsor**. Using the example in Figure 7, you can see that, in this instance, we must go three levels above the task force members to find the common boss, the executive who has line authority over all five departments illustrated here. That executive **is** the ultimate sponsor—the initiating sponsor.

I emphasize the word **is** because I write here of the reality of sponsorship in organizations. That executive, whose authority spans the organization, sponsors the work well or not well through public and private word and deed. If the sponsor's priorities are muddy or the necessary resources have not been secured or various project milestones go by unmentioned, then employees and mid-managers get the message—you can ignore this project with little risk to yourself. And if the sponsor's priorities are clear and announced, the resources properly allocated, and the project milestones are regularly monitored with widely-understood consequences for not meeting them, then another message permeates the organization—give this task force priority!

Figure 7
Sponsor-Gram

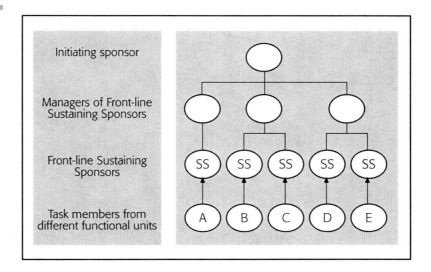

Initiating sponsor

Managers of Front-line
Sustaining Sponsors

Front-line Sustaining
Sponsors

Task members from
different functional units

The need for sustaining sponsorship is an ongoing reality, whether or not anyone ever heard of or uses the word "sponsorship." Cross-functional task groups are either left dangling with no clear support or have excellent backing, depending on the quality of sponsorship.

At the +1 stage of the Task Component scale, the Initiating Sponsor has been identified and will make the decision on outcomes, define parameters, supply resources, designate single-point accountability, and support rewards and/or reprimands. This sponsor stays connected with the team in the early defining and developing stages and in their continued progress, giving both private and public support.

Breakthrough Goals

The sponsor who can declare breakthrough goals is the one most likely to achieve success. Such a goal defines where the organization (or unit) will be in an appropriately determined amount of time. One excellent sponsor, Don Simonic, Aluminum Company of America, gave this direction: "In one year we will have reduced the cost of making our product by 20%." He also included breakthrough goals in the manufacturing process as well as the way he expected people to work together. His belief was that all of this would contribute to reduced costs. The result? In a year, his plant exceeded its cost-reduction goal.

David Helwig, Simonic's counterpart at a large electric utility announced his own breakthrough goal: "We are going to do this outage in 42 days," a project target significantly more challenging than the usual 75-day outage. His plant did it in 36 days, which was the shortest outage for a U.S. boiling water reactor in thirteen years.[19]

Both of these managers are highly successful in their respective fields. Having observed both of them in action, I cannot imagine better sponsors that these two. Both embody the concepts described here and both set breakthrough goals that

- are possible;
- stretch their people;
- are achieved in a context of concern for safety, quality, and appropriate people-involvement;
- are developed from their private experiences as well as from being continually open to the influence of others.

Both of these outstanding sponsors stay the course in the face of resistance and have remarkable ability to walk the tightrope which balances management authority with employee influence. When asked about its outage management practices by numerous other utilities, Helwig replied. "There is no technical trick. I believe it's all in management approach."[20]

SCENE VII: THE GRIDLOCK OF INDECISION

Jane and Eric are walking back from lunch engaged in a lively conversation.

Jane: "I know you're frustrated, but I need to know what you want. I'm not a mind reader, Eric. What do you need in order to succeed?"

Eric: "What I need is to be off the project."

Jane: "Come on, I can't take you off the project. Look, Eric, if you and I can get focused about our needs, maybe others will get focused and maybe the system will shift. Now what do you need?"

Eric: "All right. First, I need to know who's running this thing. Jane, we're in a gridlock right now. Everyone is blaming the 'other guy' for the delays. We're repeating behavior, making the same mistakes over and over again. Who's in charge?'

Jane: "Eric, we've been through this before. No one's in charge … well, of course, the executives … but you've got to understand that this is a cooperative effort."

Eric: "That's a very democratic sentiment, Jane, but there needs to be someone who monitors and guides this process on a daily basis."

Jane: "But that one person shouldn't make all of the decisions."

Eric: "That's not what I mean! I agree that one person shouldn't be making all the decisions, but someone should be assigned the authority to break up this log jam and keep things moving. That's what I want and need to be successful. Right now there is no one who is active in the project who has that kind of authority and Bill is too removed from the day-to-day nitty-gritty to give the leadership that is so urgently needed."

Eric has nailed the problem. Jane is still confusing authority with decision-making. Eric is teaching his boss and, fortunately, she is open to listening and learning. Shortly after this discussion, she took the issue to the initiating sponsor, Bill, who, after considerable debate and delay, gave one person single-point accountability.

SPA Chosen: +2

In the military organization model developed thousands of years ago, single-point accountability (SPA) was clear. Each unit from the general at the top down to the lowest infantry-man **knew who was in charge**! Religious and industrial organizations were developed using the same model.

That model is no longer viable in the modern cross-functional organizations where much work is done **across,** rather than **within** functional units.

Task forces, committees, projects, product development...any task involving people who do not work for the same immediate boss, are of a new order and demand new-order rules. One of the most essential rules: one person must be given single-point accountability. The rank of that person is **not** important. The authority granted for that role and person will transcend rank if the following conditions hold true:

1. The initiating sponsor actually "sponsors" as described in +1.
2. The sustaining sponsors function as described below in +3.
3. The SPA —possessing personal authority and strong inter-active skills—can **operate** with the authority granted by the organization.

Of course there is a fourth condition: **The system must know how to embrace and sustain a paradigm shift that supports** *role authority* **rather than** *rank authority.*

This is not always easy. To grant special authority to the most qualified person, regardless of rank, is a profound **emotional** shift and will be resisted. (*Most qualified* means the person with significant task and organization knowledge and the ability to operate at a high developmental stage). The sabotage will usually not be direct, but will be manifest in more subtle ma-neuvers by employees who may not even be aware of their own emotional resistance. These people might even intellectually support the idea of such SPA, admit to the bankruptcy of con-sensuality, yet still attempt to overturn decisions they oppose without seeing the contradiction. Such individuals often see a lack of egalitarianism and consensus as a moral issue. They become deeply offended by decisions that differ from their desires. They feel personally betrayed and disenfranchised when they have given input, yet find a different decision being made.

When out of touch with these dynamics, these subtle resisters attempt to explain how the decision should be reversed as if it were an **intellectual** decision and as if their opposition were rational rather than emotional. In this way, they act to undermine the authority of the SPA, even though that may not be their intention.

The primary factors determining success here are whether
- the initiating sponsor will stay the course against resistance,
- the SPA is personally developed enough not to melt when resistance surfaces,
- the sustaining sponsors are aligned with each other, the initiating sponsor, and the SPA, and
- there is sufficient ownership among those others who do the day-by-day work.

The Role of the SPA

The concept of single-point accountability is frequently misunderstood. It's not simply a clerical tracking function, nor does the SPA make all the decisions. Either extreme is the kiss of death for that role.

The person with single-point accountability is a proactive project manager who is the "point-person" about the ongoing status of the task and who insists on clarity about decision-making among the various components of the project. This person should be highly skilled as a change agent and therefore know how to ensure clear initiating and sustaining sponsorship, by-whens, and follow-through. This person knows when to handle an issue with peers and when the issue is, instead, one of sponsorship, (i.e., unclear scope, decision-making authority, roles, resource allocation, or priorities.)

Because it is not unusual for project members to be unclear about who is leading the project and what their authority is, the initiating sponsor needs to be clear in assigning single-point accountability to one individual. This decision is then communicated to all. At a subsequent kick-off meeting (described later) the primary sponsoring boss meets with the group to clarify his/her expectations.

> *"If a matrixed group is not important enough to demand such clarity or sponsorship, why have it? The intent behind identifying single-point accountability is to eliminate the black hole where **nobody** is responsible for essential functions. In a **make-it-happen** context this is empowering."*[21]

In summary, the person appointed as SPA should be fully involved and is chosen for experience and ability, not organizational rank. The highest ranking member should have single-point accountability **only** if he is the most qualified and is fully involved in the daily project work. More will be said about the SPA role later.

Sustaining Sponsors Identified: +3

The sustaining sponsors are the immediate bosses of the task force members. This may mean bosses of line managers, of non-management employees, of staff personnel who are task members, or bosses of bosses who are members. They monitor their employees' contributions on a regular basis as well as the priorities for the task group work. This is true whether or not they ever heard of the words "sustaining sponsorship" or of the concepts embodied here.

It is simply a reality of life that employees are highly influenced by the words, gestures, eye movements, and tone of voice of the person to whom they immediately report. Effective sustaining sponsors are in continuing dialogue with their employees on the project. They assure orientation and training to support the task and are willing to reward or reprimand when needed. The project will succeed or fail according to the extent that these bosses are aligned with the task and supportive of both the SPA's work and their employees' priorities on the project.

C. High Functioning Levels (+4, +5, +6)

Decision Matrix Developed: +4

If there is **no** decision-matrix or time line, then truly, no one has single-point accountability. The decision matrix facilitates movement. The time line is the schedule and the measure. (Time lines will be discussed at the +5 level). If the SPA person lacks these tools, then his functioning is severely compromised and reduced to nagging, despairing, and creating heroics. A decision-matrix is 'oh-so-simple' rationally and 'oh-so-difficult' emotionally to pull off.

The Simple

Using the chart which follows (Figure 8), list all decision issues that in previous projects have been "stuck" points. Add anticipated stuck points in the new project. For example, identify and list tasks where consensual agreements may not occur, causing delays. Be sure to include technical, budget, schedule, personnel, and procedural concerns. In addition, include previous authoritarian decisions made without appropriate consultation which led to difficult or even disastrous consequences. List these tasks in column one. In column two, indicate who will decide. Two or more people are never responsible for the same decision. Consultation is critical, but only one person's name should appear in the decision column at each possible stuck point. In column three, list those who must be consulted prior to the decision being made. In the last two columns, indicate who carries out the action and who needs to be informed.[22]

Figure 8 Single-Point Accountability Worksheet

Work Issue Requiring Decision	Who Decides?	Who is Consulted Prior to Decision?	Who Carries Out the Action?	Who Needs to be Informed?	By When?

The Difficult

Some of the previous stuck points are probably systemic issues which have been stuck points for years. If so, the organization may be utilizing the consensual decision-making style so frequently (and supposedly avoiding conflict) that **no one will decide who will decide!**

But suppose you can break this impasse. Suppose decisions are made in advance about who will decide when a future stuck point is reached. Suppose that the decision is made by the person with the greatest expertise, at least most of the time. While this tool cannot guarantee those results, it provides the framework for up-front agreements that make better decisions possible.

There will be a small percentage of decisions where executives exercise veto power, of course. They have a global, financial, strategic perspective that is critical to success.

The SPA facilitates the development of a decision matrix that is clear about who plays what roles on what issues. The decision matrix should reflect that the SPA only makes decisions in areas of her/his expertise. An engineer makes engineering decisions, a marketer makes marketing decisions, etc.

This is not about power.

This **is** about success.

SCENE VIII: THE MATRIX SEPARATES INPUT FROM DECISION

Mary is sipping coffee in the employee lounge during the morning break. Eric enters, humming a tune. He is in high spirits.

Mary: "Well, what put you in such a good mood?"

Eric: "I don't believe it, Mary. I just had a meeting with Joe. He actually asked me for input on both a decision matrix and a timeline; and get this, he made sure that I knew it was a consultation and who was responsible for the decision. I couldn't believe what I was hearing."

Mary: "What a slippery way to make you feel good and then ignore your ideas. My dad was a pro at that. He'd ask your opinion on something, and then do as he pleased. I hope you're not falling for that one, my friend."

Eric: "You're missing the point, Mary. I think Joe really listened and that the final decision will be influenced by input. I don't want to work in a dictatorship any more than you do, but I need some clarity. I'm sick of decision by consensus. It goes on and on. I want input and dialogue with others and when we disagree—which we usually do—I want someone to have the authority to decide."

Mary: "Well, good luck, Eric, but I think you're kidding yourself."

Eric: "Okay, Mary, but I think *you* need to remember that Joe is not your dad."

Time Line with Milestones: +5

An extremely helpful project management tool is the wall chart which displays the desired completion date with milestones and clarification of who will be doing what by when. A date-driven time line is the SPA's key monitoring device and the tool which drives the project. Try creating a huge wall chart for the SPA's office or, better yet, placed in the lunch or conference room. It's like a central command. A computer screen is too small to capture the dynamism of an important project.

The format of the chart can be a PERT/CPM network, a bar chart, flowchart or some combination. These may be supported by computer software when the project is large, complex, and involves interdependent activities. The by-when agreements are negotiated with one eye on speed and another eye on the reality of resource availability.

The date-driven time line is publicly known among the task force and sponsorship players.

The time line provides the details, including by-when dates for intermediate milestones, which support the target completion date. Like fabric being woven, the SPA and other project members see before them the unfolding present and the planned future.

And it is dynamic!

Work is constantly being done to achieve milestones and to adjust for previously made unrealistic plans (by increasing resources, reducing expectations, or adjusting schedules). The chart helps managers anticipate possible future missed dates early enough to shift goals or resources. The consequences of a delay between milestones on the remainder of the project becomes clear with a well-developed time line.

By-Whens

There is no commitment to action without a date for accomplishment being recorded. A major plant that had been shut down for safety reasons was losing a million dollars each day that it was closed. I attended a key daily meeting of more than thirty persons representing all facets of the daily work—engineering, maintenance, procurement, etc. During those meetings, I had two important observations:

- Participants made dozens of statements like
  "I'll do that."
  "I'll handle that."
  "Consider it done."
  "Engineering needs to get that."
  "How's maintenance doing on that?"
- But nobody recorded who would do what and by when.

So clarity about which particular person was holding the ball and authorized to act was missing. There was no single-point accountability.

Also missing was clarity about by-whens which left no tools for tracking commitments.[23] This led to nagging and pleading for action without asking for or getting clear commitments about time. People often denied having agreed to do a certain task. Blaming others—especially about their delays "causing" my delays—was a frequent occurrence. This was followed by appeals for teamwork and for each to do his part (since many apparently weren't).

To alleviate this shortfall, I asked that one member be assigned to record by-whens, review them for accuracy near the end of the meeting, and distribute them for review at the beginning of the next daily meeting. Because many commitments are softly spoken or pass quickly without most people noticing, the assigned member took a week of constant training with me at his side before he would "catch" each commitment and quickly ask for the by-when if it were not given.

It worked. Accountability was dramatically tightened with this one simple move. At least it seems so simple, yet it is a crucial management practice and essential to project success.

Surprises Are Planned For

When a competitor introduces an unplanned innovation that affects this project, how is the news handled? Who does what? Who decides any changes? If a technical task, previously seen as minor, now looms as a major problem, who does what? Anticipating these issues and deciding how to handle them up front means the project won't get mired when surprises occur.

SCENE IX: PROJECT KICK-OFF TO LAUNCH IMPLEMENTATION

Mary: "A kick-off? What are you talking about?"

Eric: "Mary, I'm sorry you're not a part of this team. It was great—everyone involved in the project was included. Some were teleconferenced, others were on speakerphones. The point is, everyone had input no matter where they were. And it worked. We actually discussed the time line and the decision matrix. We talked about what we liked and what concerned us. And we even planned follow-up sessions to talk about what is and isn't working. We may *finally* be able to keep track of things."

Kick-Off and Continuous Monitoring: +6

The project kick-off is a major event in the project life, with both substantive and symbolic value. The moment arrives. All 12 or all 1200 flow into the festivity. All are part of the drama. There is no **bit** player so unimportant as to be denied the big picture—the dream, scope, goal, roles, and strategy. This is about connection, morale, perspective, clarity, inclusion, and influence!

The initiating sponsor is there as well as sustaining sponsors. A "Sponsor-Gram" is distributed (see Figure 7), making clear the authority structure surrounding the task. The decision-matrix is shared, with all having a further opportunity for input about areas that still seem unclear. The sponsor guarantees a response to the concerns expressed and gives a by-when date. The time line is highlighted. Comments are made about the competitive issues involved in the strategy and the stretch that will be involved for all participants.

After an initial welcome, the SPA is introduced by the initiating sponsor.

> "Joe is our SPA. He has Single-Point Accountability. Now let me tell you what that jargon means and doesn't mean.
>
> He will stay on top of this project.
>
> He is the **guardian** of the time line and the decision matrix.
>
> He will know more than anyone else if the project is on track, meeting milestones, or if it is slipping. And when it appears to be slipping, he will be coming to see other task members or sustaining sponsors, whoever he needs to see to stay on track. If he needs to pull several of you together to resolve a developing conflict, he will!
>
> And if you, for whatever reason, say to him that you will not meet your deadline (with quality, of course) then you must understand that he must alert his supervisor and I expect to be alerted if his supervisor can't turn around the apparent dilemma.
>
> While I want delays solved at the source, I do not want Joe to coax, persuade, convince, or in other words act as a 'Lone Ranger.'
>
> I expect the conversation between Joe and you will be something like this:
>
> You: 'Joe, here's a warning that I'm having difficulty meeting my next deadline.'

Joe: 'Can **we** solve it?'

If the answer is **no,** then...

Joe: 'Perhaps together we could bring the problem to your boss.'

You: 'I already have and we are stuck.'

Joe: 'OK, thanks. I'll alert my boss.'

And if the sustaining sponsors can't solve the impending delay, then I want to know. The goal is success. This is not about personality differences. It is not about who's right and who's wrong. It's about making it happen!

We will not achieve long-term success if Joe ends up in a continuing persuasion role. Small wins from coaxing will not create success in the long run.

This is a systemic change, a fundamental shift in the way people believe and act. Joe's task is to stay clear about his role and not to compensate for a poorly performing system as many project managers have in the past by over-functioning, that is, by trying to do it all themselves.

We need long-lasting systemic change. We are not only going for success in **this** project but **we are creating a successful way to work cross-functional tasks in the organization!**

So, Joe, armed with this special definition of your assignment, and the decision-matrix and time line, you have a special job to do. I toast to our success! "

This 2- or 3-hour task force kick-off is then followed up in 4 to 6 weeks with another 2- or 3-hour session involving a dialogue about:

- What's changed in the external environment that affects our project?
- What's working well?
- What's the status of the schedule? the budget?
- What have we learned?

- What isn't working?
- What do we need to change?

And the best plans will break down. At that moment, the Janes and Erics of the world say, "Of course. Let's fix it." The Marys say, "I told you it wouldn't work!"

SCENE X: HONORING THEIR OWN EXPERIENCE OF REALITY

Eric: "Yesterday, seven of us from L.A. and two from London spent six hours together on a phone hook-up. Jane was there and so was Joe."

Mary: "How's this SPA stuff working out?"

Eric: "Let me finish about the meeting first, then I'll tell you. Using the old system we would have sent endless e-mail messages to one another and distributed them to dozens of other people; never meeting face-to-face and certainly never resolving anything."

Mary: "You mean to say you wasted that much time conferencing with all the *real* work there is to do around here?"

Eric: "Mary, when we were done, Louise said it felt like we got six months work done in six hours. Do you know Tom?"

Mary: "Yes ... I mean, I've heard of him. What does he do?"

Eric: "He's been trained to run difficult meetings. He ran our meeting and when it was over, our individual issues had been addressed, agreements made, deadlines set, and a follow-through session planned!"

Mary: "You sound like a religious convert. Do you really think all this will make a difference? I think you've been brainwashed."

Eric: "Brainwashed?"

Mary: "Exactly!"

Eric stops and looks at her as if he were seeing her for the first time.

Eric: "I don't think so, Mary. But isn't it funny you should mention it. I've actually had the same thought about you lately."

Mary: "What do you mean?"

Eric: "You've become so cynical that you seem... well... brainwashed."

Mary: "I'm not cynical—skeptical maybe, but not cynical. I don't like being that way, but faced with the facts as they are, it's hard not to be skeptical. You keep pretending that things are all right when they're not."

Eric: "I'll make a deal with you, Mary. You and I have worked next to one another for more than two years. Our conversations have always been important to me. But there's something I've just realized that disturbs me. I've always given into your skeptical side to the point where I felt guilty about being optimistic. What I realized is that your facts aren't necessarily facts, they're opinions. I value your opinions, but I won't view your skepticism as my reality any longer. Here's the deal, Mary. From now on, I'm staying true to my current experience. As an example … I feel great about these meetings and at this point I even have some renewed hope for this company. How does that grab you?"

Mary: "Fine with me, but understand that I'll be staying true to my experience also. I'm going to maintain my role as realist. You can go live on a cloud if you want. I will give you one thing. I'm surprised at how many people say that your project seems to be working. It won't last long though. I just don't want you to set yourself up for a disappointment."

Several days later . . .

SCENE XI: RIDING THE PROJECT LEARNING CURVE

Eric is working at his computer. He has a smile on his face as Mary enters.

Mary: "Hey, Smiley."

Eric: "Hi, Mary."

Mary: "Judging from the look on your face, things must be going pretty well. Everything's beautiful, right?"

Eric: "Cut it out, Mary. If you really want to hear how it's going, I'll be glad to tell you."

Mary: "Oh, all right. How's all this SPA stuff working out. You were asked that before and you didn't answer."

Eric: "Well, SPA has had a rough ride. You see there was an SPA in each department but not an SPA who had authority over all. So, things got bogged down. Joe was finally assigned as total project SPA. Not long after that, he started acting like a dictator, making decisions that weren't his to make on the decision chart. Many of us got irritated and called a meeting to iron out our differences. "

Mary: "Sounds like chaos to me."

Eric: "Not really. All the project members ..."

Mary: "Wait a minute, did you say all?"

Eric: "Yes, everyone ... we all meet every month and assess what is and what isn't working. You may find this hard to believe, Mary, but by meeting at prescheduled times we actually save time. For example, we're running about two weeks behind schedule on this current project, but have you ever known a project of this size in this company that was only two weeks off schedule?"

Mary: "No, I haven't. If you keep this up and stay close to your target... well, I may become a believer myself."

Eric: "We don't need believers, Mary. We just need people who hang in and keep going for clarity."

Eric hit the nail on the head with his simple rule for project success—hang in and keep going for clarity! When people are using high interactive skills and are supported by task-clarifying tools, success is possible. The degree of success hinges on one crucial factor—the health of the overall system.

Chapter 4: **Rating The Health of Your System**

"The system is the solution."

—W. Edwards Deming

The skill stage of the SPA and the degree of task component clarity will be for naught in the long run if the system is and remains unhealthy. In my winning formula…

Project Success = (LISS + TC) x SH

the skill stage of the SPA is added to task-component clarity but is **multiplied** by the overall health of the system. While an over-functioning project leader may pull off an occasional short-term win, forces in an unhealthy system will continually influence the organization to return to the familiar unless the system shifts. "Project failure often stems from organizational failure."[24]

In my previous book, *Walking the Empowerment Tightrope*, I both examine the components of high-performance system health and suggest ways to improve. Figure 9 contains a summary of twelve key system dimensions drawn from that book and their status in both healthy and unhealthy systems. The "Rate Your System Health" questionnaire describes these characteristics.

Figure 9
Characteristics
of Healthy and
Unhealthy
Systems

Dimension	Unhealthy System	Healthy System[25]
Management	Frantic	Centered
Influence	None	Appropriate
Alignment	Not well aligned	Well aligned
Communication	Gossip—closed	Openness and dialogue
Consequence management	Capricious discipline	Clear consequence
Decision-making	Consistently extreme (either consensual or authoritarian)	Flexible and clear
Interactive Skill	Low	High
Task Goals	Unclear	Clear
Accountability	Fuzzy	Single-point
Implementation	Poor	Effective
Rewards	None	Appropriate
Sponsorship	Poor	Clear

Of course, low system health scores will blunt positive scores in LISS or TC. In this situation, somebody has to be concerned about strategies for system change. You may achieve success and slowly influence the larger system, but this rarely happens without a strategy that engages other key persons in the system. What follows is a tool that can be used individually or by project teams to diagnose their systems along these twelve dimensions. Here are some ideas for use by the team:

1. Distribute the "Rate Your System Health" questionnaire and have each person do their individual ratings,

2. Draw the horizontal grid 0-10 on 12 separate flip chart pages,

3. Go through the 12 dimensions one at a time, beginning with *a* (management). Poll each member for their numerical ranking and put a check mark above the corresponding number. With all the check marks up, you'll see the distribution of rankings.

4) After each set of rankings, discuss and write the notable responses on the flip chart

   - What causes the rankings to be where they are?
   - Is each dimension sufficiently healthy to support our project?
   - If not, what can and should we do?

Finally—and perhaps most importantly—invite each member to "Speak from the I" about what they can do. The following are some examples.

   - "I will ask for clarity about decision responsibility when I am unclear about who's deciding."
   - "I will interrupt a meeting if I don't understand what's going on and ask for clarity."
   - "I will speak to my sponsor about areas of sponsorship that are not working."
   - "I will ask for 'by-whens' (who will do what and by when) and also give such commitments."
   - "I will go directly to someone when I'm troubled instead of talking about them to others."
   - "I will, as a sponsor, keep in constant communication with the people who are working for me."

5. Have someone capture action ideas and by-whens. Share the results of this meeting with the initiating sponsor and be specific about the support you need from him or her. (More about this later.)

Figure 10
Rate Your
System Health

(Circle one)

	LOW SYSTEM HEALTH						**HIGH SYSTEM HEALTH**				
a.	0	1	2	3	4	5	6	7	8	9	10

Fire fighting from incident to incident; frantic management is the norm.

Unless the incident is a rare occurrence, it is examined as a pattern and something is done to change the pattern thereby reducing the number of old recurring fires to fight.

b.	0	1	2	3	4	5	6	7	8	9	10

People affected by and/or those who have the most experience about the issue being discussed are never consulted prior to decisions being made

The appropriate people are in dialogue prior to the decision being made with clarity that being consulted is not equivalent to making the decision.

c.	0	1	2	3	4	5	6	7	8	9	10

Our people seem at odds with each other.

While retaining the ability to share differing ideas we, as an organization, seem aligned and headed in the same direction.

d.	0	1	2	3	4	5	6	7	8	9	10

Gossip is the way of life. People do **not** talk directly to the person with whom they differ.

If people disagree or feel irritated, they speak directly with each other, hang in, resolve the issue, and heal the work relationship.

e.	0	1	2	3	4	5	6	7	8	9	10

Resistant and/or poor performers run this organization. Those resisting don't simply talk about objections but they persist. Sometimes this means that nothing seems decided and an impasse continues. Management seems helpless in the face of these people.

There is clear consequence management. Resistance is heard - dialogue is typical but not prolonged and then it is made clear what is expected and, if necessary, consequences for ongoing resistance.

f.	0	1	2	3	4	5	6	7	8	9	10

Consensus or authoritarianism is in. Consensus is manifest by the attempt to change already-made decisions (not as a rare attempt but a predictable pattern), lack of clarity about who decides, pretense that we all decide, the frequent question, "Who decided that?" and an egalitarian philosophy. Authoritar ianism is manifest by a pattern of decisions made without appropriate influence by those impacted.

Flexible decision-making is in with clarity about the decision-making process. Appropriate persons give input in a listening environment with dialogue about the issue at stake. Decision is made by the previously identified decision-maker.

g.	0	1	2	3	4	5	6	7	8	9	10

Low interactive developmental behavior (as described previously in this book) is the normative behavior of management.

High interactive developmental behavior is the normative behavior of management.

h.	0	1	2	3	4	5	6	7	8	9	10

Task goals are typically vague.

Task goals are typically clear with appropriate flexibility.

i.	0	1	2	3	4	5	6	7	8	9	10

Accountability is out! No one seems accountable.

Accountability is clear.[26]

j.	0	1	2	3	4	5	6	7	8	9	10

Poor implementation history.

Excellent history of implementation on time, with quality, and on budget.

k.	0	1	2	3	4	5	6	7	8	9	10

No rewards for success, no incentives, no thanks, no celebrations, no money ...nothing.

Appropriate tangible and intangible rewards.

l.	0	1	2	3	4	5	6	7	8	9	10

Poor sponsorship. Maybe a rah-rah speech, maybe not, but nothing else by way of support.

Clear sponsorship: organization aligned around clear goals and priorities, consequence management, appropriate monitoring, resources allocated, goal-related rewards.

System Change Is Difficult But Not Impossible

Difficult as it is, when the system is functioning poorly, fundamental change is essential. Organizational restructuring is often an attempt to solve perplexing matrix problems. While the change may be more positive than negative, restructuring is no answer for poor sponsorship or lack of health. Further, the new structure usually leaves in its wake a trail of unclarity about goals, roles, priorities—indeed dysfunction in all twelve system health areas identified here.

All change primarily engages people's **emotions**. While clear **thinking** is required to identify leverage points in, for instance, the twelve system issues identified earlier, change almost always requires unexpected behavior shifts, even on the part of those who most want the change. Change is primarily a "gut" issue rather than a "head" issue.

The capacity to implement and sustain shifts toward system health are more difficult than the ability to analyze, conceptualize, and plan for change. The likelihood of a "Lone Ranger" shifting a system is extremely low. The key elements in successful change are to:

1. Be clear about where you are headed.
2. Be clear about what price you are willing to pay. If you are ready to lose all, to quit or be fired, your chance of success is higher.
3. Examine your other life options so as not to become desperate in your pursuit of the change.
4. Speak from the "I" position. Don't blame. Take responsibility for your own beliefs and goals. Be clear, but don't persuade.
5. Find a sponsor. Without sponsorship, you will likely fail. You may be stoned, as have been many advocates.

Change advocates who are great blamers end up **creating** new enemies by their accusations, thereby encouraging polarization. Rather, educate your newly found sponsor to use her positional leverage to advocate a system change among the twelve system health factors and others specific to your organization that you identify.

Concentrate on ways that you can change patterns. Systemic change will not happen by focusing on isolated events. Rather, look for what encourages those events as part of a dysfunctional pattern. Then, initiate actions that shift the patterns.

How to change patterns and implement systems that sustain effectiveness is the million-dollar quest. I've written this book for the reader who is:

- *Operating at a high interactive skill stage.*

  Clarity about your own wants, the ability to be connected, and the capacity to deal with resistance without blaming are more important than the other profile dimensions.

- *Living personal values that are compatible with the organization.*

  You can't be happy long-term if the values of your organization are at odds with your own. Give serious thought to finding an environment where you can live a congruent, integrated life.

- *Interdependent with authority.*

  You're right if you think this is a characteristic of the high developmental stage. It is! And it needs highlighting.

  You must believe that authority simply is, and that it is inherently neither good or evil. Authorities, indeed all employees, must function with clarity for good ends to ensue.

- *An advocate for change.*

  If yes to the above, this book is written for you.

The most powerful gift you bring to your situation is your non-anxious, non-blaming presence with clarity of goal and determination to not give into resistance. The following planning outline summarizes key elements of your strategy for achieving success.

Write here the project goals, major milestones, and the completion date.

Check task component items not yet effectively in place.

_____

_____

_____

_____

_____

_____

_____

_____ _Initiating Sponsor_

_____ _SPA_

_____ _Sustaining Sponsors_

_____ _Decision-Matrix_

_____ _Time-line with by-whens_

_____ _Kick-off...¬_

_____ _Plans for follow through sessions_

List restraints that prevent your organization from receiving higher system health scores _(from the twelve System Health questions, plus others you may add.)_

_____   _____

_____   _____

Next, with your sponsor, begin to discuss the system restraints **as habitual patterns**. _Illustrate their occurrence. Apparently the patterns, though dysfunctional in many ways, have some positive payoff for someone, otherwise they would not persist._

What are these?

Whom do they benefit?

_____   _____

_____   _____

_____   _____

Apparently, there is more **pain** associated with changing the patterns than with keeping them the same as always. What would you need to do, allied with your sponsor, to reverse this? Outline a strategy allied with the sponsor. Remember that the sponsor can only sponsor those who are his/her direct reports. Likely your project will demand sustaining sponsorship and employee support from many parts of the organization. Your sponsor may need to become an advocate in search of other sponsors. The proactive advocate role will not be successful without getting sustaining sponsorship in place. You cannot **coax** change, or **will** change. And you will not succeed with sponsors unless they are experiencing some pain with the present task component process or with the projected lack of results.

SCENE XII: CLARITY LIBERATES ENERGY

Eric: "You know, Jane, early in this project I was frustrated, confused, and near the burnout stage. I didn't know what to do. But now I'm working just as hard as ever. Sometimes I'm frustrated, but I *know* what to do!"

Jane: "Eric, please don't burn out on me now!

Eric: "Don't worry, Jane. I'm very busy, but I'm working on my priorities. Before, most of my energy got sucked up in that black hole of confusion."

The task is important. Perhaps very important. But not of **fatal** proportions.

When you find yourself triggered into defensive postures again and again, having sleepless nights, losing your center, being an anxious rather than a non-anxious presence most of the time, and feeling emotionally like this is a life-and-death issue, you may be fighting a losing battle. The best strategy in this case may be to quit the battle.

Actually, achieving personal clarity about yourself and your goals may be the most important **force** in changing organizational patterns and systems.

SCENE XIII: DIFFERENT STROKES FOR DIFFERENT FOLKS

Eric is seated at his desk packing his briefcase. Jane enters his cubicle.

Jane: "Hi, Eric, are you ready for the long weekend?"

Eric: "You bet! These last few weeks have been stimulating but I need a change of pace."

Jane: "What happened with your friend Mary?"

Eric: "She's still around, but she has a much different view of life than I do. Her world seems full of hopelessness. She and I used to talk a lot but we don't any more … do you know the poem 'I met her and we never met?'"

Jane: "No."

Eric: "The poem describes our relationship to a 'T':

> *'I met her and we never met;*
> *We looked and had no sight.*
> *Our time together seemed to pass*
> *Like ships on foggy night.'*

Her world seemed a lot like my world here before this project. It's strange... we talked, but didn't talk. We work in the same company, but don't. I experienced a shift while on this project and she didn't. I'm sorry she wasn't on the project too. I met her and we never met. I feel sad about that."

Eric didn't know how to "stay connected" with Mary. Once he refused to continue criticizing the organization, he lost this ally. Functioning at a higher skill stage does not guarantee success. These are not techniques, but a profoundly different way to be. Likewise, task component clarity will be met with resistance. There is no easy way. There is the hard way of task and personal confusion or the hard way of task and personal clarity. There is the hard way of giving up on system health or the hard way of attempting to influence the system toward greater health.

There is no guaranteed way. But there is a more contented, less anxious way. That way begins with clarity about myself, where I am headed, how I will get there, and above all, how I will nourish my core being, my integrity. And when I do that, my energy will be freed for creativity, my work life will be enhanced, and my organization will be lucky that I am there.

$\mathcal{N}otes$

1. Tom McCombs was the Personnel Director at the ALCOA Addy, Washington, plant from 1975-1992. He graduated from the LIOS/ Leadership Institute of Seattle's graduate program in Applied Behavioral Science in 1980. LIOS was founded in 1969 by the author.

2. Crosby, R.P., *Walking the Empowerment Tightrope: Balancing Management Authority and Employee Influence.* (King of Prussia, PA: Organization Design and Development, Inc., 1992). This book was influenced by and completed during our work at the ALCOA Addy, WA plant.

3. Built in the mid-1980s, Volvo's Uddevalla plant was designed as a "human-centered" organizational model giving work teams substantial latitude in how they performed their tasks and authority over what have traditionally been higher-level management decisions. Critics say this organizational design fostered a management philosophy that was more like abandonment than empowerment. The plant was closed in late 1992. See P. Adler and R. Cole, "Designed for Learning: A Tale of Two Auto Plants," *Sloan Management Review*, Spring 1993, pp. 85-94.

4. *New York Times*, March 20, 1991.

5. While this scale has been designed by the author, it rests on the shoulders of Kurt Lewin whose system formula was mentioned in the *Acknowledgements* of this book on page v. His student, Dr. Ron Lippitt was a mentor of the author for over two decades.

6. This is a quote from Dr. Ron Short, The Leadership Group, Seattle, WA. Ron was one of the original faculty in 1973 of the LIOS graduate program along with the author and John Scherer who resides in Spokane.

7. P. Senge, *The Fifth Discipline* (New York: Doubleday, 1990). See pp. 238-249 for an excellent exposition of the difference between discussion and dialogue. Senge acknowledges his debt to the late quantum physicist David Bohm who significantly developed these ideas in his writings and personal dialogues.

8. Such training is available bi-yearly through Crosby & Associates (www.crosbyod.com). The training is called "Emotional Intelligence at Work" (Also called "Tough Stuff") and is open to all who want to improve their skills. They also hold trainings internally in locations throughout the globe. Internal trainings net the greatest gain because the leader and their employees raise the overall skill level of the organization together.

9. D. Williamson, *The Intimacy Paradox* (New York: Guilford Press, 1991).

10. T. Weber, "Seeding and Harvesting: Redefining Success and Failure," Publication for the Leadership Institute of Seattle/LIOS.

11. T. Weber and F. Levine, "The Art and Craft of Engagement: Beginning with the Family," a chapter in *Family Psychology and System Therapy*, Miksell, Lustoman and McDaniels, eds. (Washington DC: The American Psychological Association, in press).

12. Senge (1990).

13. R. Short, *Creating Your Learning Culture*, (Seattle, WA: The Leadership Group).

14. E. Freidman, *Generation to Generation*, (New York: Guilford Press, 1985).

15. The People Performance Profile, developed by John Scherer and the author provided data from 600 organizations.

16. Crosby (1992), p. 2.

17. Crosby (1992), p. 3.

18. C. Berggren, "NUMMI *vs. Uddevalla*," Sloan Management Review, Winter 1994, pp. 37-46.

19. Nuclear News, May, 1994.

20. *Ibid.*

21. Crosby (1992).

22. *Ibid.*

23. *Ibid.*, pp. 18-19, 64-68.

24. Schmidt, T. (1992) *Planning for Successful Project Implementation.* Management Concepts International, Seattle, WA.

25. Crosby (1992). See particularly the 25 High Performance factors derived from research and experience in 600 organizations.

26. In a restrictive system, people fear clear accountability. In a creative system, clear accountability is empowering: "I know what is expected of me and my authority to act."